Body Art

TATTOOING

Paul Mason

Heinemann
LIBRARY

www.heinemann.co.uk/library
Visit our website to find out more information about **Heinemann Library** books.

To order:
☎ Phone 44 (0) 1865 888066
📄 Send a fax to 44 (0) 1865 314091
💻 Visit the Heinemann Bookshop at www.heinemann.co.uk/library to browse our catalogue and order online.

First published in Great Britain by Heinemann Library,
Halley Court, Jordan Hill, Oxford OX2 8EJ, part of Harcourt
Education. Heinemann is a registered trademark of
Harcourt Education Ltd.

© Harcourt Education Ltd 2004
The moral right of the proprietor has been asserted.

Editorial: Lucy Thunder and Helen Cannons
Design: David Poole and Kamae Design
Illustrations: Kamae Design
Picture Research: Rebecca Sodergren and Elaine Willis
Production: Edward Moore

Originated by Repro Multi-Warna
Printed and bound in China by South China Printing
Company
The paper used to print this book comes from
sustainable resources.

ISBN 0 431 17922 0
08 07 06 05 04
10 9 8 7 6 5 4 3 2 1

British Library Cataloguing in Publication Data

Mason, Paul
Tattooing. – (Body art)
391.6'5
A full catalogue record for this book is available from the
British Library.

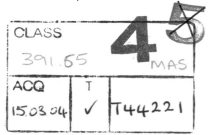
Acknowledgements
The Publishers would like to thank the following for
permission to reproduce photographs:

AKG Images p**23**; Ancient Art and Architecture/Ronald
Sheridan p**25**; Art Archive/Naval Historial Services,
Vincennes, France/Dagli Orti p**20**; Camera Press/Chris
Ashford p**5**; Camera Press/Martin Godwin p**6**; Corbis/Dave
Bartruff p**27 bottom**; Corbis/Natalie Fobes p**22**;
Corbis/Catherine Karnow p**13 top**; Corbis/Paul A. Soulders
p**4**; Corbis/Patrick Ward p**19**; Corbis/Bettman p**13 bottom**;
Corbis/Stapleton Collection p**27 top**; Corbis Sygma/La Venta
p**7**; C.M. Dixon p**9**; Hulton Archive pp**8**, **10**, **14**; Hutchison
Picture Library p**15**; Andreas 'Curly' Moore p**26**; Rex Features
pp**16**, **17**, **29**; Rex Features/Brendan Beirne p**18**; Rex
Features/Phanie Agency p**24**; Rex Interstock Ltd/Richard
McLaren p**11**; Topham Picturepoint p**28**; Werner Forman
Archive/Auckland Institute and Museum p**12**.

Cover photograph of a Maori with *moko* facial tattoos,
protesting at the Waitangi Day celebrations in New Zealand,
reproduced with permission of Corbis/Paul A. Souders.

The Publishers would like to thank Jenny Peck, curator at the
Pitt Rivers Museum, University of Oxford, for her assistance
in the preparation of this book.

Every effort has been made to contact copyright holders of
any material reproduced in this book. Any omissions will be
rectified in subsequent printings if notice is given to the
publishers.

CONTENTS

Words appearing in bold, **like this**, are explained in the Glossary.

TATTOO WORLD

The first tattoos

When was the first tattoo done, and who wore it? It was a long time ago, certainly: **mummified** bodies from 4000 years ago carry evidence of ancient tattoos. These tattooed mummies include ancient Egyptians, **Pictish** warriors from Scotland, an early Alpine traveller, the priestess of a long-dead Siberian religion and plenty of others.

Of course, these may not have been the first tattooed people – they may just be the first ones we know about. Tattoos are permanent markings that are made underneath the top layer of a person's skin. If the skin rots after death, as it does on most bodies, evidence of the tattoo disappears. So tattoos may have been around for even longer than 4000 years – but there is no definite evidence to prove it.

This Maori man from New Zealand wears moko *tattoos on his face. In the past, this style of tattooing was extremely painful, and caused the face to swell up so much that it was impossible to eat. Instead, people sucked liquid food through a straw for several days, or even weeks.*

Tattooing today

Tattooing has never been as popular as it is today. Walk along any street, in any city, in any country – you will see a huge variety of tattoos coming towards you. In London in the UK lots of people will be sporting **Celtic**-style tattoos – big, single-coloured shapes with lots of points and sharp edges. In Tokyo in Japan you might catch sight of an intricate tattoo poking out of the wrist of a man's shirt – he may be a **yakuza**, a member of the Japanese **underworld**, with his whole body covered in tattoos that have taken years to finish. In Auckland in New Zealand you could run into a **Maori** man whose face has been tattooed in a traditional style, with each swirling pattern carefully designed to suit his features. In San Francisco in the USA a group of motorcyclists hanging around outside a café might have tattoos showing the bike club they belong to or the kind of motorbike they prefer to ride.

People have tattoos done for lots of different reasons. It might be to show membership of a club, or to mark a significant moment in their life (the change from being a girl to being a woman, for example). Some tattoos are done as a sign of love, or as a reminder of an important event or person. Often, people have a tattoo simply because they think it looks good.

Like many other people, Melanie Griffith has the name of her husband tattooed onto her arm. Other Hollywood stars have come to regret tattoos like this one.

'Tattoos are symbolic of the important moments in your life. Talking about where you got each tattoo and what it symbolizes is really beautiful. They're like stories.'
Actress Pamela Anderson, who has since had at least one of her tattoos altered

Permanent designs

Tattoos are made by putting a dye of some sort into the layer of skin called the **dermis**. Unlike the outer layer of skin, the dermis does not get rubbed away and replace itself over time. Colour that is added to it stays almost exactly where it is for as long as the skin is alive. For this reason, tattoos are essentially permanent.

Around the world and through history, people have made tattoos using various different methods. The most common today is the use of a needle to prick through the skin. If the needle is coated in ink or some other dye, some is left behind in the dermis when the needle is pulled out. Enough of these tiny pinpricks made next to one another allow the tattooist to create lines and coloured areas, and even to create shading.

In some places, tattooists have used knives, sharpened seashell or even chisels to cut through the outer layer of skin. Colour is then added through the cut, which seals up over the tattoo. Once the cut is fully healed and the scab has fallen off, a coloured line is left where the cut was made.

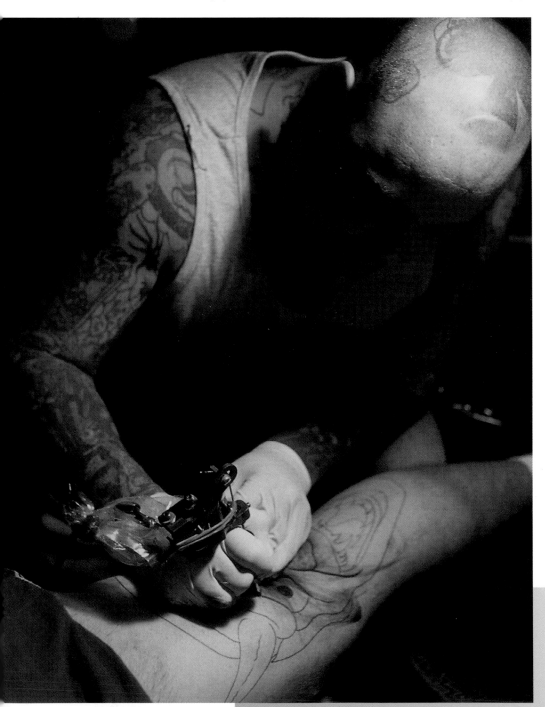

TATTOOING PAIN

Most people agree that having a tattoo is painful. Some say the pain was mildly uncomfortable, others wept and wailed when they had their tattoo done. Gillian Anderson, the X-Files actor, had a tattoo done in Tahiti. She later said that 'it felt like I was at the dentist and they were drilling into my bone.'

This tattoo artist is using a modern, electric-powered tattooing device. The first such machine is said to have been based on the 'Electric Pen' invented by Thomas Edison in the 19th century.

This tool used for tattooing was found by a geographical team exploring Mexico's Cueva del Lazo. The Cueva is a canyon which contains artefacts believed to be about 6000 years old.

Another tattooing technique was used by, among others, the Inuit peoples of the Arctic. Their culture had developed by AD 1000 in the Bering Sea region, between Alaska and Russia. They would soak a thread in soot or ink, then use a needle to draw the thread under the skin. A trail of colour was left behind as the thread passed through the dermis.

The tattoo machine

Most tattoos today are made using special machines. The first tattoo machine was invented in 1891 by Samuel O'Reilly, in New York, USA. It used a needle that went up and down like a woodpecker's beak. Each downward stroke carried a small amount of ink with it, piercing the skin and leaving the ink behind. Modern tattooing machines work in a similar way – they are faster than older methods and more **hygienic** if used properly.

Tattoo removal

Tattoos can be removed, but the process is very expensive. **Lasers** are used to **vaporize** the colours, which then spread out and disperse around the body. A tattoo that cost about £30 to have made would cost roughly £480–720 to have removed using lasers.

Tattoo safety

Because of the possible health risks involved in getting a tattoo, it is important to make sure they are done in the safest way possible. The most important thing is to go to a proper tattoo studio. These use specialist cleaning equipment and trained staff, reducing the risks to a very low level.

PROFESSIONALS VERSUS AMATEURS

Having a tattoo done by an amateur – a friend, or someone's older brother, or even yourself – is a bad idea for three reasons:
1 It will probably be painful, as amateur tattooists often dig too deep and go through the dermis into the flesh.
2 It will not turn out right, as few amateur tattooists have access to the transfers that professionals use to make sure they get the shape right. Nor do they understand how tattoos will be affected by the skin stretching.
3 It is unlikely to be hygienic, as few amateurs have access to an **autoclave** for cleaning equipment.

! Safety

See page 30 for more information on safety and tattooing.

'Anyone considering a tattoo should keep in mind that removal is painful, takes multiple procedures, requires ... anaesthesia and is expensive.' Dr Jerry S. Dover, Harvard Medical School

ANCIENT TATTOOS

The beginnings of tattooing

It is impossible to be sure how people discovered how to make tattoos. Somebody accidentally falling on a sharp, burned piece of wood might well have discovered tattooing. Once the wound healed they could have noticed that the black mark left behind by the burned stick had remained. But people have been modifying their bodies in various ways for thousands of years, through piercing, scarring and painting. So it is equally possible that someone with a deep cut was then painted, and that the paint washed off everywhere except the cut, leaving a tattooed line.

Knowing when the first tattoos were done is also tricky. Skin **decomposes** after death, so evidence of tattooing does not usually exist once someone has died. Their skin rots away and the evidence of their tattoo disappears. Because of this our knowledge of ancient tattoos comes from three main sources. The first is **mummified** bodies, where the skin has been dried out before it has time to rot. The second is ancient written accounts of tattooed people. Finally we get evidence of tattooing from objects that people left behind them, showing they had tattoos: these include paintings, drawings and models.

Tattoos from the Ancient World

The first evidence of tattoos (though not necessarily the first tattoos) comes from ancient Egypt. Tomb drawings and models of ancient Egyptian people seem to show that between 4000 BC and 2000 BC, people living in the Nile Valley began to tattoo themselves. Figures found in the tomb of an ancient Egyptian ruler called Seti show people with tattoos on their arms and legs.

This outlandish couple are a figment of an artist's imagination: the ability to shade tattoos to look three-dimensional has only existed worldwide in modern times.

'They mark their bodies with various figures of all kinds of animals and wear no clothes for fear of concealing these figures.'

Ancient Roman historian Herodian, writing about the Picts of Britain in the first century AD. Herodian was wrong to think that the Picts did not wear clothes, but they may have stripped off for battle.

Otzi the Ice Man

In 1991 the mummified body of a man was found high in the European Alps, lying almost across the mountainous border between Italy and Austria. The man, who has since been nicknamed Otzi, had not died recently. He was actually over 5000 years old, and had been mummified by the cold, dry conditions in the mountains. His skin bore evidence that he had been tattooed, making his tattoos as old as those worn by ancient Egyptians.

This detail of the tattood arm of a Scythian chief dating from the 5th century BC shows fantastic beasts.

HOLY TATTOOS

This passage from the Book of Leviticus in the Bible's Old Testament was often used by Christian **missionaries** as a reason for banning tattooing: 'Ye shall not make any cuttings in your flesh for the dead, nor print any marks upon you: I am the Lord.'

Until recently Christians frowned on tattoos, and in the 18th and 19th centuries Christian missionaries tried to stamp out tattooing among **indigenous** peoples around the world. But in fact tattooing has played an important role in Christianity. In the past priests based outside the walls of the city of Jerusalem made tattoos, usually of the cross, for **pilgrims** to take home as proof of their visit to the holy land.

The tattooed priestess

Other evidence of ancient tattoos comes from Siberia, where in 1993 the mummified body of the priestess of an ancient religion was discovered. The 2400-year-old mummy wore bright-blue tattoos of animal figures. These probably represented the creatures her people would have killed for food, and the tattoos may have helped her ensure good luck for the hunters.

This tattooed priestess may have been a far-flung relative of the **Pictish** peoples who fought the Romans in northern Europe about 2000 years ago. They too tattooed themselves with blue figures, mainly of animals, and were said to look very terrifying in battle when they stripped naked to charge at the enemy.

THE PACIFIC ISLANDS

'Tattooing neither covers nor disfigures the body, but rather blends in with it in graceful adornment and seems to enhance its beauty.'
Adalbert von Chamisso, who visited the Marshall Islands in 1816–17

Pacific patterns

Tattooing has a long history in the islands of the Pacific. The patterns used are very distinctive, and vary from place to place. Normally the tattoos are made using just one colour, a dark blue or black. The tattooing colour is applied to the skin in complicated patterns, featuring dots and a combination of wavy and straight lines. Often the tattoo is adapted from a traditional design to suit the person who is having it done.

Throughout the Pacific, and certainly in places such as Tahiti and Tonga, almost everyone once wore tattoos. An early French explorer remembered that 'the women of Tahiti dye their loins and buttocks a deep blue.' Tattoos were usually applied using a painful technique that involved coating a sharpened comb-like device in colour and tapping it into the skin.

Design influences

One of the most distinctive forms of tattooing was done in the Marshall Islands. Tattoos here drew their inspiration from the sea – the local word for tattooing, 'eo', is the same as the word for a fish covered in lines that resemble tattooed marks.

During the 19th century one visitor to the islands said that the fully tattooed men looked 'as though they were dressed in a chain mail suit.' Each tattooed mark represented some element of the natural world, usually something to do with the sea. For example, tattoos might stand for the markings of fish, tooth marks made by fish bites, or shells.

This picture, probably owing much to the artist's imagination, shows someone from the Marquesas Islands. Colour for tattoos was usually a black substance made from the soot of burned candlenuts.

The death and rebirth of tattooing

In much of the Pacific tattoos were outlawed by Christian **missionaries**, who began to arrive there shortly after the first traders, in the early 1800s. The local people were persuaded or forced to follow the Christian religion and told that their traditional beliefs were no longer good. By the early 20th century, traditional tattooing had largely died out, and young Pacific islanders began to have Western-style tattoos.

Traditional tattoos have now become popular again in parts of the Pacific. In Tahiti the old techniques have been made illegal because they are **unhygienic**. So, using new tools, dozens of tattoo artists are now giving people traditional or near-traditional designs. A young Tongan named Aisea Toetu'u is reviving the ancient style of tattooing. Aisea and his wife have tattooed his whole body in imitation of a famous drawing of a Tongan man's tattoos made by an early French explorer.

HAWAII

In Hawaii, traditional techniques and styles of tattooing are making a comeback. Hawaiians used tattooing to show strength, express sadness (usually by tattooing the tongue) and humiliate defeated enemies. By about 1830, Christian missionaries had succeeded in wiping out tattooing in the Hawaiian Islands. One type of traditional Hawaiian tattoo that survived longer than the others was a saw-toothed ring that looked like shark's teeth around women's ankles. It protected its wearer from attack by a real shark.

Today, traditional patterns from the skins of **mummified** Hawaiians, sketches made by early European visitors and other sources are being used as the basis for tattoos. More and more people are getting tattoos in designs that were last worn almost 200 years ago.

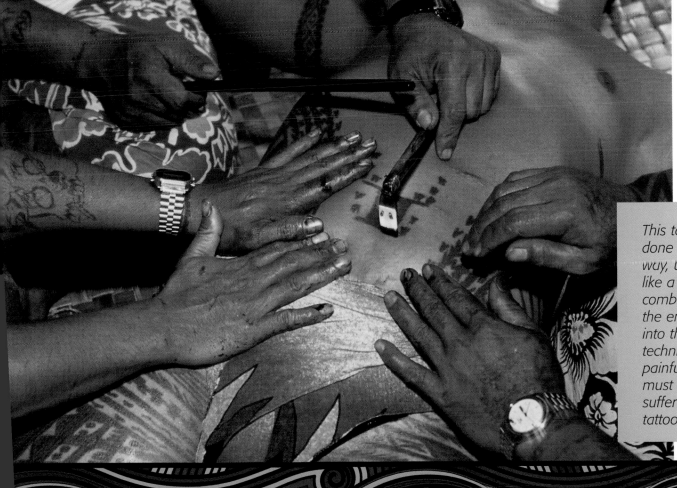

This tattoo is being done the traditional way, using a device like a tiny chisel with comb-like teeth on the end to tap ink into the skin. The technique is very painful. This man must already have suffered for the tattoos on his legs.

MAORIS AND SAMOANS

Maori tattoos

The **Maori** people of New Zealand traditionally tattooed both their bodies and their faces. Face tattooing was known as *moko*, and may have reflected the rank of the person wearing the tattoo. Women had small tattoos on their lips and chin, while men had complicated swirling patterns covering their whole face. Each tattoo was adapted specially to suit the features of the person having it done.

These facial tattoos were extremely painful. The tattoo was done using a chisel with a serrated edge made of bone. The chisel was coated in colour and then used to carve the design through the skin's outer layer, into the **dermis**. Because of the terrible facial swelling caused by this process, it was impossible to eat proper food for some time. Instead people ate liquid food through tubes until the swelling had gone down.

When Europeans arrived in New Zealand, Maori tattooing began to die out. The Christian **missionaries** who reached the country in the late 1700s thought the tattoos were 'ungodly', and discouraged people from having them done. However, during the 1970s facial tattoos began to appear again as pride in Maori culture began to grow stronger. Some Maoris today paint their faces to resemble the old-style tattoos, but an increasing number are also having the designs permanently inked into their skin.

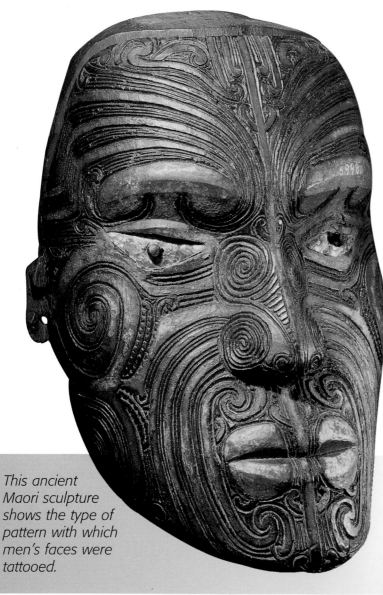

This ancient Maori sculpture shows the type of pattern with which men's faces were tattooed.

CAPTAIN COOK

The famous English explorer, Captain Cook, visited the Pacific Islands on his 1769 voyage. Tattooing had practically died out in Europe by this time, and the journey bought many of his sailors into contact with it for the first time. Many seamen took home a permanent reminder of the voyage in the form of a tattoo. Word spread, and soon many more sailors wanted tattoos – this was the start of tattooing's increase in popularity in the West. Tattoos have been popular with sailors ever since. This sailor is having a tattoo done in a tattoo parlour in the USA in the 1940s.

This photo shows the hip and wrist tattoos of a Western Samoan chief. The tattooed area has raised skin, caused by scarring, because the tattoos have been made in a traditional manner.

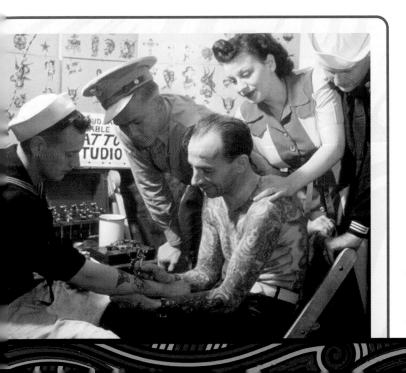

Samoa

Before Christian missionaries arrived in the Pacific in the late 1700s and early 1800s, Samoan tattoos were used as body decoration. Because they were painful to have done, they served as a badge of 'toughness' among Samoan men. The designs are complicated and could take months to finish, partly because the method Samoans used for tattooing was quite slow. First, a special comb with sharpened teeth was made. The teeth of the comb were dipped in ink, then tapped into the flesh using a small hammer. The teeth were withdrawn, leaving behind an even amount of ink in each hole. Some accounts say that the tattoos were applied in a specially built hut. Once the tattoo was finished the hut was burned down.

FACT
....
The word 'tattoo' almost certainly comes from a Tahitian word, *tatau*, which means 'to mark'.
....

JAPAN

'The men of Wa [the ancient Chinese name for Japan] tattoo their faces and paint their bodies with designs. They are fond of diving for fish and shells. Long ago they decorated their bodies in order to protect themselves from large fish. Later these designs became ornamental.' From *Gishiwajinden*, a 3rd-century Chinese history book

Japan's first tattoos

In 1977 a set of clay figures called *dogus* were discovered near Osaka in Japan. The *dogus* were incredibly ancient – probably about 2500 years old, in fact. The little clay figures appear to have tattoo marks on their faces and bodies, suggesting that Japanese people have been wearing tattoos since at least 500 BC.

Tattooed criminals

By about AD 700, however, tattooing had begun to be seen as a bad thing. A book called the *Nihonshoki* (which means 'Chronicles of Japan') says that a criminal called Azumi no Murajihamako was tattooed as a punishment for his crimes. Tattooing continued to identify criminals for hundreds of years. For **bribery**, **extortion** and **swindling**, a tattoo of a black line was made around each arm, or sometimes a **kanji** was tattooed on the criminal's forehead.

Ukiyo-e

Despite that fact that criminals were often tattooed, ordinary people continued to have tattoos done as well. Their tattoos were more elaborate and done in a very distinctive style.

The most painstaking and elaborate style of tattooing in the world comes from Japan. These are tattoos done in the same style as Japanese *ukiyo-e* paintings. *Ukiyo-e* means 'floating world'. The name comes from the period of Japanese history when this style of painting became popular. The lines and shading of these tattoos makes them more like paintings than the flat colours of, for example, the Pacific Islands or **Celtic**-style tattoos.

This picture shows a guild, or group, of gamblers, wearing traditional tattoos that reach from shoulder to foot. The clothed central figure is the chief of Japan's gamblers, Umezu.

People also liked to be tattooed with scenes from a set of Chinese stories called *The Water Margin*. The characters in *The Water Margin* were heroes who helped the poor and weak. People's favourite character, Kyumonryu Shishin, had tattoos of nine dragons. Many Japanese had dragon tattoos like his. *Ukiyo-e* tattoos were first done on people's backs, but soon they spread over the shoulders and arms until some people had practically their whole body covered in one interlinked tattoo.

Yakuza

Yakuza are Japanese criminals a bit like the Mafia in the USA and Italy. They control many of the illegal activities that take place in Japan, including things such as drug smuggling and illegal gambling. The most obvious trademarks of a *yakuza* are his tattoos. Some *yakuza* have tattoos covering their whole bodies, ending only at the wrists, ankles and neck, with a small V-shaped gap at the top of their chest left bare so that they can wear an unbuttoned shirt without the tattoos being seen. Mainly because the *yakuza* are associated with crime, full-body tattoos are frowned on in modern Japanese society.

Today

Today many young Japanese, like young people everywhere, want to have tattoos. But instead of the traditional style that covers large areas of the body, they often have 'one-point' tattoos. These are single images like those that are popular in Europe and North America. There are now different words in Japanese for the two styles – *wabori* for the old style and *yobori* for the Western style.

This photo shows a Japanese yakuza *gangster. Some people claim the first full-body tattoos were made as imitations of fine fabrics. Tattoos were popular because the rulers of Japan had banned ordinary people from wearing fine, colourful clothes. Instead of wearing fashionable clothes, they coloured their skin with fashionable shapes and colours.*

SCRIPT TATTOOS

Meaningful tattoos

In recent years tattoos that use foreign **scripts** – especially Japanese *kanji* and **Hindi** script – have become increasingly popular in Europe, Australia and North America. People like the way these tattoos can pack a lot of information into a small space. The *kanji* for 'love', for example, can fit into a space not much larger than a thumbnail. Hindi script and religious symbols also pack a lot of meaning into a small space.

Kanji tattoos

Kanji tattoos are everywhere. They are sported by a huge variety of people: musicians, football stars, basketball players, actors and, of course, people in the street. What are these tattoos, and what makes them so popular?

WHAT ARE KANJI?

Kanji are part of a Japanese writing system, which uses symbols that are completely unlike the letters used in the West. These symbols were imported to Japan from China and then adapted to suit the Japanese language. *Kanji* started life as simple pictures – for example, of a house. Over time, the same type of picture of a house began to be used by everyone who wanted to make a note of 'house'. Then the picture got more and more simplified until, in lots of cases, a *kanji* no longer looks anything like the thing it is supposed to represent.

Kanji come from a Japanese writing system that uses stylized drawings of things to show meaning. *Kanji* can be used together to create new meanings from old words. So, for example, the *kanji* for 'electricity' and 'car' are put together to mean 'train' – a kind of electric car. There are about 50,000 *kanji* all together, but most of these are only used very rarely. To read a newspaper people only need to learn about 2500 symbols; Japanese children have to know at least 1945 *kanji* before they leave school.

Celebrities who sport kanji *tattoos include Mel C from the Spice Girls (whose mum has the same 'Girl Power!' tattoo), actor Taye Diggs and Marcus Camby of the New York Knicks basketball team.*

Hindi tattoos

Tattoos that use the Hindi writing script from the Indian subcontinent are becoming increasingly popular. Like *kanji* tattoos, the meaning of these is usually hidden unless the wearer chooses to tell people what it says. Among the stars sporting Hindi tattoos are the England footballer David Beckham, who has his wife's name written on his forearm.

Why do people have script tattoos?

To answer this question you have to think about why people have tattoos at all. Someone with a tattoo risks being looked on with dislike: it can make it harder to get a job, a girlfriend or boyfriend, or even just to make friends with new people. So getting a tattoo needs a lot of thought and planning. People usually want to have something that is important to them tattooed on their skin, and it needs to be something that will be important for years to come, rather than the name of their current favourite pop group or clothing label. Script tattoos are good for this because only the person wearing it usually knows the meaning of a script tattoo. This makes the tattoo a little personal secret, with a meaning just for its owner and anyone they care to let in on the knowledge.

NATIVE AMERICAN TATTOOS

Historical records

Unfortunately there are few reliable records of the types of tattoo that **Native American** people wore before Europeans reached North America. Many of the first Europeans to arrive noticed that the people they met wore tattoos, but they rarely recorded what the tattoos looked like. One **missionary** who travelled through eastern Canada in the middle of the 17th century did give some idea of the designs he saw:

'They [Native Americans] trace images of animals or monsters. For example an eagle, a serpent [snake], a dragon, or any other figure they like, which they engrave on their faces, their necks, their chests, or other parts of their bodies.' It seems likely that the tattoos he saw were influenced by the natural world, and the spirit creatures and animals that are part of Native American culture.

NATIVE AMERICAN THEMES TODAY

Today tattoos with Native American themes are popular across the world, but especially in the USA. Among the people who wear Native American-themed tattoos is the actor Mickey Rourke, who has a bull's skull with four feathers hanging from its horns on his right arm. Apparently this tattoo was originally used by the Zapotec people, who lived in what is now Oaxaca in Mexico from about 1500 BC to AD 750. The tattoo was used to mark out a **shaman** who repeatedly interpreted people's dreams wrongly. As well as a longhorn skull tattoo (shown here), musician Jon Bon Jovi has a Superman sign on his left bicep.

Buffalo skulls are favourite subjects for tattoos with a Native American theme, but people also wear the heads or full figures of Native American warriors, **totems** and representations of animals from the Pacific North-west.

'In order to paint permanent marks on themselves [Native Americans] undergo intense pain ... [Tattooing] is so widespread that I believe that in many of these native tribes it would be impossible to find a single individual who is not marked in this way.'
Jesuit missionary Francois Bressani in 1653

Just as they did when they arrived in other parts of the world, Christian **missionaries** quickly persuaded or forced many people to give up their cultural traditions. This included tattooing, which most Christians thought was forbidden by the Bible.

Tattoo techniques

We do have records of how painful the tattooing process was. Among the Huron people, who lived in what is now eastern Canada, the sharpened bones of birds or fish were used to puncture the skin. Gabriel Sagard-Théodat, a French explorer, wrote in 1615 that: 'During this process they exhibit the most admirable courage and patience … they remain motionless and mute [silent] while their companions wipe away the blood.' Then a black colour or powder was rubbed into the cuts, and the scab left to dry and fall off. In other tribes a needle, sharpened **awl** or thorns were used instead of sharpened bones. Having a tattoo done was a risky business: one missionary wrote that 'many have died after [being tattooed], either as a result of a kind of spasm which it produces, or for other reasons.'

Tattooing seems to have been common among many Native American groups. Along the Mississippi river, for example, the Acolapissa, Houma, Chickasaw and Chitimacha peoples all wore tattoos. Some peoples limited tattooing to just men; in others both men and women had tattoos. Both body and face tattooing were used. Tattoos were also worn by Native Americans who lived on the Great Plains, in the Pacific North-west, the far north and the desert south-west.

Today, traditional patterns from sketches made by early European visitors and other sources are being used as the basis for tattoos. More and more people are getting tattoos in designs that were last worn almost 200 years ago.

American bikers have traditionally worn tattoos, often based on Native American cultural images. This biker has many different images all over his body.

SOUTH AMERICA

'[The Amerindians] make bloody incisions [cuts] in their chests, arms and legs. They then rub black powder into the incisions, which makes them indelible [impossible to wash off] ... Those with the most scars are given the greatest respect.' Jean de Léry, *History of a Voyage to Brazil* (1577–78)

Amazonian tattoos

Many of the first Europeans to explore South America mention the tattoos worn by the **indigenous** peoples. One of these was a Frenchman named Henri Estienne, who actually took some **Amerindians** back to Europe with him, to show them off at the French court. It seems unlikely that he asked the Amerindians whether they wanted to come, so they were probably forced to leave their homelands. Estienne wrote a book about his travels in 1512. In it he said that the native people sometimes had faces and bodies that were covered in scars and tattoo marks.

Other explorers also mention these marks. Often they claim that the marks were linked to **cannibalism** – that people either had the marks to show how many others they had eaten, or in preparation for going out and catching a victim. These reports were probably untrue. Few early explorers knew enough of the local language to understand what people were saying.

This drawing was entitled Native of Brazil, *and first appeared in a book published in 1633. The man seems to have many tattoo marks all over his body.*

Patterns and techniques

Amerindian tattoos were made by cutting into the skin, then rubbing some sort of colour into the cut. Sharp rocks, thorns and the teeth of fish or small animals, among other things, were used for cutting. Some peoples seem also to have used pointed sticks to make dotted tattoos on their skin.

As soon as Christian **missionaries** arrived in South America, they began to discourage people from having tattoos. The traditional patterns and techniques quickly died out, although they may survive deep in the rainforest among some unknown tribe.

Street tattoos

As South America's cities began to grow in the late 19th century, a new form of tattooing became popular. Many of South America's people are **devout** Catholics and many of the tattoos that began to be made featured religious images. Tattoos of Christ on the cross, the Virgin Mary, people's favourite saints and other religious images started to become extremely common.

There were few of what we would today think of as proper tattoo studios then. In Rio de Janeiro most tattoos were made by small boys of about ten to twelve years old. They used just a bottle of ink and three needles attached to a stick. The boys walked the street asking people 'You want a mark?' They often earned more than a grown man did working for a whole day.

'Lucky Tattoo'

One of the key people in Brazilian tattooing was a Danish sailor called 'Lucky Tattoo'. He opened a tattoo shop in 1959, and not long afterwards did a tattoo for a surfer named Petit. One of Petit's friends wrote a song about him, which described his tattoo – a winged dragon. The song became a massive hit, and suddenly everyone wanted a tattoo like Petit the surfer's. New tattoo studios sprang up everywhere.

The winged dragon remains a popular tattoo design today.

Tattooing today

Today, tattooing among South Americans is more influenced by what is going on in the rest of the world than by Amerindian styles. People like Japanese-, **Celtic**- or Pacific-style tattoos, just as they do in New York, Sydney or Paris. Tattoos with religious themes are still more popular in South America than in other places.

RIO LADIES

In the early 20th century, women in Rio de Janeiro used to have the initials of their boyfriends tattooed over their hearts.

If they split up with the man, they would then have his initials tattooed on the soles of their feet. That way, they could step on him forever!

Tattoo history

Tattooing has an ancient history in the world's Arctic regions. Arctic peoples include Native Americans, Laps from Lapland and Greenlanders and they are spread over a vast geographical area. A 3500-year-old carved figure shows that even so long ago – at the time of ancient Egypt – Arctic peoples were tattooing themselves. In the 1970s, a **mummified** woman with tattooed forearms was uncovered when a beach on St Lawrence Island wore away. **Carbon dating** showed that she had been buried in the sand for about 1400 years.

Tattoo styles

Traditional tattooing styles were similar right across the Arctic region, including the Yupiget people of St Lawrence Island, Inuit people in Canada, Alaska and Greenland, and Chukchi people in Siberia. Although there were differences between these groups, there were many similarities in the style and use of their tattoos.

Tattooing was most common among women, although men were also very likely to be tattooed. Women typically had their faces tattooed in a number of different places.

CHIN TATTOOS

Anthropologist Sergei Bogojavlensky said that one of the reasons for women having chin tattoos was that 'it was believed that a girl who smiled and laughed too much would cause the [tattooed] lines [on her chin] to spread and get thick. A girl with a full set of lines on the chin, all of them thin, was considered to be a good prospect as a wife, for she was clearly serious and hard working.'

These two Inuit ladies are wearing traditional face tattoos, which were probably done when they were very young women.

Their foreheads could have a V-shape, made up of two lines running down from near to the hairline to the top of their nose. On each cheek might be an egg-shaped tattoo running from their nostril to the outer corner of their eye. The most common tattoo decoration for a woman, though, was a stripe of lines or patterning on her chin. Some people say that this stripe was there so that it was possible to tell women from men, as bundled up in their cold-weather gear it was almost impossible to tell any other way! Whether this is true or not, almost all females had the tattoo to mark the change from being a girl to a woman.

Men were also tattooed, usually with dots or lines on their joints. Some hunters also had whale flukes (the two halves of a whale's tail) on their face, or circular tattoos at each corner of their mouth (see page 25).

Technique

Arctic tattoos were usually made in one of two ways. People in some regions used a needle to pierce a hole under the skin. Then a thin piece of pine that had been coated in dye was passed through the hole. In other regions, a needle was used to pull a thread of **sinew** under the skin. The sinew was coated in dye, some of which was left behind as the thread was pulled through.

Tattooists in the Arctic were almost always women, and usually they were older women. This may have been because these women would have been very skilled with their hands. After a lifetime of sewing clothes, gloves, kayak shells and a huge variety of other things from the skins of various animals, they would certainly have been good at using a needle and thread.

Fact

The dye used in Arctic tattoos was made of a mixture of lampblack, urine and graphite.

This drawing was made by explorer John Ross on an expedition from 1829 to 1833. It shows tattoo marks on the women's faces.

23

HEALTH TATTOOS

Preventing illness

In some parts of the world tattoos have been used as a way of warding off illness or protecting people from other kind of harm. In the Arctic, for example, people thought that illnesses and conditions such as **rheumatism** were caused by imbalances in their **souls** – usually these imbalances were caused by evil spirits. Parts of the soul escaped, or the evil spirit entered their body, through their joints. Tattooing designs on the joints could block them off, stopping the leaking-out of the soul that lead to illness.

The Iban and Kayan peoples who live in Sarawak (part of Borneo in Malaysia) also used tattoos as a way of preventing illness. They thought that when a person was ill their spirit left their body, and only returned when the person was well again. To prevent the spirit escaping, people at first wore a bead tied around their wrist. Over time the bead was replaced with a tattoo of the bead. The tattoo was thought to fend off illness.

Acupuncture tattoos?

One old Yupiget Inuit woman remembered her grandparents tattooing people to make physical problems go away. 'Grandparents, when they were [tattooing a point to stop someone] hurt from a headache, or when they thought the eyes were bothering you … they use an **acupuncture**.' Acupuncture is the use of thin needles inserted into the skin to improve health. Many of the tattoos used by Arctic peoples to stop illness are in the same place as acupuncture points.

Protective tattoos

Other Arctic tattoos were used to protect against mishaps. These 'guardian' tattoos could be used to save people from disasters at sea, help them on a journey through unknown territory, or even guard against the death of a new child. One of the main risks for Inuit hunters out on the ice was that a walrus might attack them.

This woman is having acupuncture, an ancient Chinese treatment for a variety of health problems. The locations on the body of some traditional tattoos are located on acupuncture points, raising the possibility that they may have had health benefits.

Whale-fluke tattoos, like these men's, were thought by Inuit people to protect a man from danger while he was out hunting. They also showed he was becoming a successful hunter.

People who lived around the Bering Strait (between Alaska and Russia) thought that walrus which had been left motherless when they were very young were the most likely to attack humans. These walrus had not been taught properly that they were meant to eat molluscs and seaweed.

To protect themselves from walrus attack, men would have small circular tattoos under each corner of their mouth. These tattoos echoed the white marking on the side of a killer whale's head. As a killer whale could easy kill even a large walrus, the tattoos protected the hunters from attack.

ARCTIC TATTOO MEDICINE

Examples of how tattoo marks were thought to cure particular illnesses on St Lawrence Island include:
- a mark over the chest-bone, which was placed there to cure heart trouble
- a small line over each eye, to cure eye problems
- guardian tattoos included a small circle under each corner of the mouth, to protect a man against falling into the sea and drowning
- circles or half-circles were tattooed in special places on people's arms and legs to protect them from particular diseases.

CELTIC TATTOOS

Modern-day Celts

Tattoos done in a **Celtic** style are among the most popular of the last few years. All around the world people wear these distinctive-looking tattoos. Some of them are modern-day Celts: people who live on the north-western fringes of Europe, in Scotland, Ireland, Wales, Cornwall or Brittany. Others are the descendants of people from Celtic lands, whose families have moved to other parts of the world – the USA, Australia or New Zealand, for example. Often they want to remember their roots by having a Celtic-influenced tattoo.

Of course, Celtic tattoos are not just worn by people from a Celtic background. Plenty of other people have them too, including music stars like Keith Flint of The Prodigy, who has a mixture of Celtic and tribal designs on his legs, and Mel C of the Spice Girls, who has a Celtic cross on her left arm.

Tattoo inspiration

Inspiration for today's Celtic tattoos does not actually come from tattoos the ancient Celts wore. Instead, most designs are based on patterns found in **illuminated manuscripts** that were made in Ireland from about AD 600 onwards. In those days printing had not been invented. Each book was painstakingly put together by individual craftsmen, who wrote each word separately.

Many modern-day Celtic tattoos are inspired by the Book of Kells, which is said to be one of the most beautiful illuminated manuscripts in existence. The book survives to this day, and is kept in the library of Trinity College, Dublin, in Ireland.

ANCIENT PICTS

Like some Celts, the Picts lived on the northern fringes of Britain. The Picts were given their name by the Romans, who first wrote about them in about AD 297. The Roman word for 'painter' is *pictor*: the fierce tribes the Romans met in the north-east of their empire tattooed their bodies with blue ink, and ended up being known as Picts. Because the Picts did not leave written records of their culture, there are very few descriptions of what their tattoos looked like. They seem likely to have been mainly animal shapes, which may have had some sort of religious significance. Other peoples who tattooed animal shapes on their bodies often did so to help them in their hunting activities or to protect them from harm by dangerous animals.

As decoration, intricate paintings were added by painters known as illuminators. Like the tattoos of the ancient **Picts**, these paintings often featured animals. They also showed complicated interlaced patterns of knots and spirals.

Other inspiration for modern-day Celtic tattooists comes from things the Celts left behind them: pottery, jewellery, sculpture and architecture. Many tattooists are inspired by the patterns found on old Celtic crosses. In Ireland, for example, carved crosses stood in front of most churches and in the spaces between monastery buildings. Many of these survive today, and some tattooists have taken rubbings of their patterns to use in tattoos.

Some tattoos are inspired by the religious designs associated with Christianity, especially those carved in churchyards and on crosses at the roadside.

This modern tattoo is very similar to one that the Celts would have worn, with interlaced patterns.

Modern Celtic tattoos

Two main forms of Celtic-style tattoo are popular today. The one you are most likely to see on the arm of someone walking towards you is the Celtic cross. This is a cross shape containing complicated interlaced patterns. Other shapes use similar interlaced designs – sometimes these are worn as a band around someone's arm, or in a disc shape or even a rectangle. The looping patterns have no start or finish; instead they swoop in and out without ending.

COSMETIC TATTOOS

Permanent beauty treatments

Cosmetic tattooing is different from the tattooing that is featured on other pages of this book. Most tattoos – **Celtic** ones, for example, or Pacific Island tattoos – are done as a form of body decoration. They are almost like a painting that has been permanently marked on someone's skin. Cosmetic tattoos are done to blend in with a person's natural features, more like wearing make-up than wearing a painting. People have cosmetic tattoos for two main reasons: to cover up some sort of problem with their skin, such as a scar, or because they cannot or do not want to wear make-up.

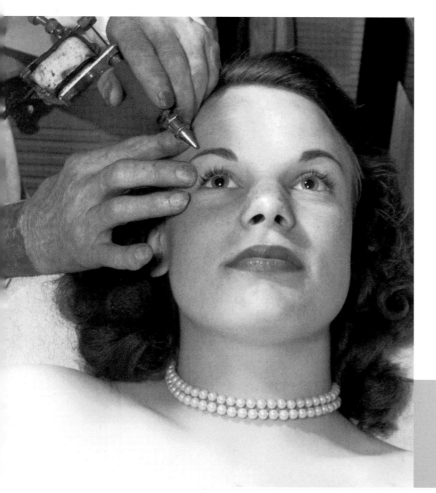

One of the first people to practise cosmetic tattooing was a man named George Burchett. In the early 1900s Burchett, who had tattooed members of various royal families, began to work in a beauty salon in London's Piccadilly. At this time it was thought very unladylike to wear make-up – which was only worn by actresses on the stage and other 'low class' women. But at the same time, the fashionable look for women was to have healthy-looking, flushed cheeks. How to get this look if you were pale-faced but would not wear make-up?

The answer lay in Burchett's salon. There, some of the smartest, richest ladies in London had subtle colour added to their cheeks. Though the actual word was never used (the service was advertised as a 'permanent beauty treatment') they were in fact having facial tattoos. This kind of cosmetic tattooing became less popular when it became more acceptable for women to wear make-up.

Casualties of war

After both World War I and II, many men came back from the fighting with terrible scars and burns. Burchett worked alongside the doctors to help these war victims return to a normal life. Ink from his tattoo needles was able to bring back skin colour to burned areas, and to make scarring far less noticeable than it had previously been.

'Professor' George Burchett applies a permanent tint to a young woman's eyebrow. Burchett, who left school in his early teens, was known as 'Professor' because of his great skill at tattooing.

'The word 'tattooing' was never mentioned.' George Burchett remembers when he first began to give ladies cosmetic tattoos (*Memoirs of a Tattooist,* 1958)

Cosmetic tattooing today

Cosmetic tattooing is again becoming popular today. Skilled tattoo artists are able to provide women, in particular, with permanent eyeliner, eyebrow outlines and lip colouring. Cosmetic tattooing is now sometimes called 'micro-pigmentation' or 'dermal pigmentation'.

Cosmetic tattooing is also being increasingly used to disguise or reduce the effect of scarring, especially as a result of surgery. For example, women who have had one or both of their breasts removed because of cancer sometimes have new breasts surgically constructed.

Another example of the new uses of cosmetic tattooing comes after someone has had a facelift. Some people who have these are left with scarring around their ears where the surgeon has cut. This pale scarring can be tattooed so that it blends in with the surrounding skin.

In a similar way, tattooing can be used to help victims of car crashes, fires and other accidents. Even people who have been born with discolouration of their skin can be tattooed to reduce the effect.

WARNING!

In many places the authorities do not regulate cosmetic tattooing. Much cosmetic tattooing is done on the face, where any mistakes would be disastrous. Because of this, anyone thinking about having cosmetic tattooing done should check the tattooist's qualifications. Speak to people who have had a similar treatment and make sure they are happy with it. Ask to see 'before and after' photos of treatments, too. Ideally, get a recommendation from your family health practitioner.

Some people use tattooing to completely transform themselves. Eric Sprague, the 'Lizard Man', has been tattooed and surgically altered to look like a lizard. Over half a century before this, George Burchett tattooed a man named 'The Great Omi' to look like a zebra.

Safety tips

In most countries, the legal age limit for having a tattoo done is eighteen; this is the case in the UK and Australia. Even where there is no age limit, many tattooists will not tattoo non-adults, for fear of being taken to court for assault. This is the common charge in the USA for tattooing someone aged either under 18 or 21 without parental agreement.

Anyone getting a tattoo needs to be sure that it is done hygienically. This is because tattooing can cause bleeding, and there is a risk of blood-borne diseases such as hepatitis and HIV being passed on. There are a number of ways to reduce the risks:

! Always go to a professional tattoo studio with a storefront. The people there should be happy to explain the process; if they are not, it is best to walk away.

! Make sure that the tattoo studio has an autoclave (a device for cleaning equipment at very high temperatures).

! Check that the ink, ink cups, gloves and tattoo needles are fresh and new. These pieces of equipment are disposable and should not be used more than once.

! Once finished, tattoos must be kept dry as much as possible, but also kept clean with antiseptic soap. Pat the tattoo dry; rubbing it can cause the colours to smudge.

Books

Body Piercing and Tattooing, Paul Mason (Heinemann Library, 2002).

Celebrity Skin: Tattoos, Brands and Body Adornments of the Stars, Jim Gerard (Apple, 2001).

Memoirs of a Tattooist, George Burchett (Oldbourne, 1958).

The Body Art Book: A Complete Illustrated Guide to Tattoos, Piercings and Other Body Modifications, Jean-Chris Miller (Berkeley Publishing Group, 1997)

Websites

http://www.tattoo.com
All sorts of interesting snippets and essays.

http://www.howstuffworks.com
Excellent information about how tattoos are made and how to make sure they are done hygienically.

http://www.safe-tattoos.com
The home site of the Alliance of Tattooing Professionals, dedicated to raising standards of hygiene and professionalism among tattooists.

http://www.japan-guide.com
This site has information about the history of *kanji*, Japanese writing characters.

http://www.japaneseculture.about.com/bltattoo.htm/
This site allows you to get a *kanji* name for your tattoo.

Places to visit

The Pitt Rivers Museum in Oxford, UK, the Victoria and Albert Museum in London, UK, and The National Costume Museum, Lobethal, Australia, may all have tattoo-related exhibits from time to time. So will other regional museums – check your local newspaper for listings, or look in the national listings pages of daily newspapers, which often have this information on Saturdays.

Glossary

acupuncture use of small, thin needles to treat illness. The needles are carefully pushed through the skin at specific points on the body: where they are placed depends on what illness is being treated

adornment decoration

Amerindians people descended from those who lived in South America before Europeans arrived there

anaesthesia medical substance that causes loss of feeling in all or part of the body

anthropologist person who studies the ways in which different human societies around the world work

archaeologist person who studies history by digging up and studying items left behind by people in the past

assault attack someone physically

autoclave machine that uses high temperatures to clean tattooing instruments

awl tool like a large needle with a wooden handle that is used to make holes

bribery making a dishonest payment to someone as an unfair way of influencing their decision

cannibalism human beings eating each other

carbon dating scientific technique for measuring the age of very old objects

Celtic relating to people who were originally from the north-western fringes of Europe, especially Wales, Ireland and Scotland

cosmetic any product used to make the body or face more beautiful

decompose to rot away

dermis the inner layer of skin, into which tattooing colours are placed to make a permanent pattern

devout especially active in following a religion

extortion forcing someone to give you money through the use of threats

hepatitis blood-borne disease that causes inflammation of the liver, pale skin and fever

Hindi relating to a group of spoken dialects from northern India

HIV an incurable virus. People who have HIV usually develop AIDS, a disease that can reduce the body's resistance to infection and lead to death.

Holy Land parts of the Eastern Mediterranean based around the city of Jerusalem, where many holy sites of Christianity, Judaism and Islam can be found

hygienic clean and healthy

illuminated manuscript handwritten text that is illustrated with colour paintings. The paintings often weave their way around the first letter of a new chapter or paragraph.

indigenous describes people who are originally from a place: for example, Aboriginies

kanji Japanese writing system that uses symbols instead of letters

lampblack the powdery carbon left behind by burning some fossil fuels, for example oil in an oil lamp

lasers powerful beams of light that are able to burn through objects

Maori person descended from the people who lived in New Zealand before Europeans arrived there

missionary person who travels to a foreign place to try and persuade people to join his or her religion

moko Maori tradition of facial tattooing

mummified preserved after death through drying out

Native American descendant of the peoples who lived in North America before European settlers arrived

Pict member of an ancient people from Scotland

pilgrim person travelling to a holy site for their own religious reasons

prehistory time before written records and recorded history

rheumatism disease that affects the joints of humans, making them inflamed and sore

scripts styles of writing

shaman person from a society with spiritual powers, who plays a leading role in their community

sinew the tough, strong band of material that joins muscle to bone

soul person's mind or spirit

swindling cheating someone out of something

symbol/symbolize a symbol stands for, or symbolizes, an idea

totem natural object, especially an animal, adopted by Native North Americans as a symbol of a clan or of an individual

underworld secret criminal world or society

unhygienic unclean so that illness or infection may be likely

vaporize to turn into vapour, the visible gas form of a liquid (for example, steam from boiling water is water vapour)

yakuza Japanese group of organized criminals who run many of the illegal activities in Japanese society

INDEX

Titles in the *Body Art* series are:

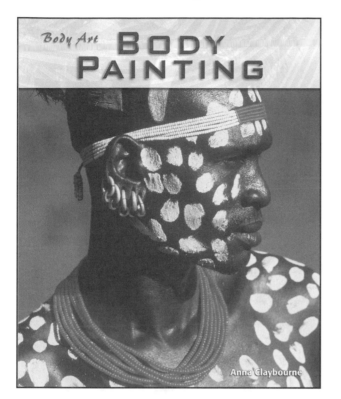

Hardback   0 431 17923 9

Hardback   0 431 17925 5

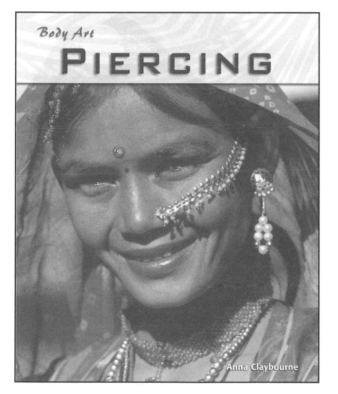

Hardback   0 431 17924 7

Hardback   0 431 17922 0

Find out about other series by Heinemann Library on our website www.heinemann.co.uk/library